BREAK THROUGH

Shakisha Edness

BREAKTHROUGH Volume II

Copyright © 2014 by Shakisha Edness

Published by T.R.A.C Publishing

Cover design: Jacobie Brown

Editor: Shanice Edness

Cover illustration: Google and Shutterstock

Interior illustration: Google and Shutterstock

Interior design: T.R.A.C Publishing

Bible Scriptures: New Living Translation

Definitions: Webster's Dictionary and Google

ISBN: 10: 0692025391

ISBN-13: 978-0692-02539-0

Library of Congress catalog card number:

Printed in the United States of America

DEDICATION

THIS BOOK IS DEDICATED TO MEN

I thank you for purchasing this book, sowing a seed into my life, as I am being used by God to sow a seed into yours.

I wrote two books titled *BREAK THROUGH*. One book speaks directly to men and the other is designed for women.

But when God initially spoke to me about this book, it was created just for men. As God began giving me revelation for both partners, I was excited to have a word for women as well. I am honored to be used by God.

Please buy *BREAK THROUGH* Volume I for your fiancé or wife, because it will ignite the fire into the relationship and the fire will burn forevermore.

Blessings and Miracles...

A personal special dedication to the following men in my life, that I want to see God allow a Break Through to take place in their lives individually, collectively, and generationally.

Larry Riley, "The moment we reconnected, I realized everything that was missing in my life was you. The very fiber of your being lives within me and I thank God for you daily." **Unconditional...**

Sidney Smith Jr., "You are the reason something tangible came out of the seed that you planted in me as a little girl. That was the seed of teaching me to set goals and reach them. Aim high baby girl and jump higher!" **Motivational**...

Elliot Alexander Jr., "You are the picture perfect of restoration. Over the years, I have seen the hands of God restore you mentally, emotionally, physically, socially, spiritually, and financially. You have instilled in my daughters, that nothing beats a failure but a try. They were an extension of you to me." ***Inspirational***...

Tamajain Gilyard Edness, "You have always told me to make my own decisions and stick to them. In making my own decisions, they have cost me a lot but paid me even more. But I thank you because I do not suffer the consequences of others decisions, but of my own." ***Responsibility***...

Shakim Edness, "We have always had a bond that is not easily broken. That bond is a brother and sister's love for one another. There is absolutely no other word that describes us, I love you greatly." ***Unity***...

Richard Gibbs Jr., "You are my Gift from God, that is not deserved but well appreciated!" ***Irreplaceable***...

To my grandsons, *Zy'kee Padilla* and *William Garcia* Jr., "You are both examples of God's ways and thoughts not being like man. I prayed for change and he sent both of you." ***Purpose***...

Xavier A. Mosley, "You are a constant reminder of what you have instilled in our daughter and in me. That nothing remains the same. Your best is yet to come!" ***Newness***...

Robert E. Reid, "You are truly the person who God used to teach me the true meaning of forgiveness. I forgive you in Jesus' Name." ***Freedom***...

Richard Gibbs Sr., "You taught me to never give up!" ***Persevere***...

CONTENTS

ACKNOWLEDGEMENTS

I thank God for allowing me to read His word and allowing His word to come alive in me like never before. Therefore, enabling me to release it to His people and watch Him do as He said. I thank Him for speaking to me, through me, and for me. This is a story that I read that truly blessed me in a way that I will forever be thankful to God.

I sincerely and wholeheartedly thank my daughter and editor, Shanice Edness, for the time sown into editing my books (eight to ten hours at a time). You cannot imagine how much I appreciate you. Many turned me away, because I could not financially afford them. Others rejected me, because they did not believe in my dream. A few individuals thought I was their competition. But God! He sent someone that could afford to be a blessing to someone else. And not take the credit, but give Him the Glory that belongs to Him. May every seed sown boomerang back into your life thousand fold.

Jacobie Brown, my graphic designer, friend, and whom I call my son. You have truly been a blessing in disguise. I cannot find the words to express how great you have been to me. You have been up with me in the late night hours, working on projects when you knew I had nothing to give in return. You constantly said, "Momma, no worries. I am sowing seed." I pray God open His floodgates, breaking every barrier, allowing the seeds sown to spring forth a harvest that you won't have room enough to receive.

I thank many for praying for me, believing in me, and supporting me.

Reginald Leonard, "Thank you for always calling and standing in the gap for me by constantly praying with me and for me."

Adrian Manning, "The way God has spoken through you during this process, has truly kept me focused and helped me to refocus."

Also, I would like to give thanks to a man that I love dearly. I can still remember when I called him and asked him if he had previously said there was a man midwife in the bible. He responded, "No." I then asked, "Well, what did you say your middle name was?" He said, "Perez." I asked, "What does it mean?" He said, "Break Through. Read Gen 38:28-30."

The funny thing is that I was already reading Genesis 38, but I was at the beginning of the story. I had not yet made it to the end, so when he directed me to that story I made sure I read the entire story. I marveled because instantly God spoke to me announcing, *"BREAK THROUGH!"*

On May 18, 2013, the day of my birthday, I attended this man's graduation. He was a country boy from Alabama and the ninth child born of his siblings.

He is the first of all to graduate in his family. He attended the military service, moved to Atlanta, and continued his education in college at Strayer University in Douglasville, Georgia. This man was determined to break through the barriers, obstacles, excuses, and the generational curses in order to tap into the generational blessings for himself, his family, and the generations to come.

He has a career, a home, a car, and most of all a relationship with Christ.

His testimony spoke to my life and it is part of the reason for this book being written as well. He has been a blessing to me and has silently encouraged me to pursue my dreams as an Author.

Blessings O.P.B.

God used him to help me deliver what was in me, this is my *Break Through*!

INTRODUCTION

Are you praying for a breakthrough? Have you heard the pastor or the prophet say a breakthrough is coming your way? Have you yet received it?

Have you been told your wife is barren? Did the doctor say that she will never be able to birth children of her own? Do you believe God can speak life to her womb and allow a baby to come forth? You do? Amen, keep reading.

Do you complain that your wife is lazy, she does not cook or clean, and she barely gives you sex? Does this sound familiar?

What is barren?

Barren is incapable of reproducing; unproductive. To reproduce is to copy or duplicate; to propagate. Propagate is to breed or multiply; to spread or extend.

Man of God, have you planted something into your wife, for her to birth out? Have you given her something to work on lately? Are you planting on fertile ground?

This does not necessarily mean a baby, but your vision or dream. Have you shared your vision with her?

Be honest with yourself. After seeing the cover of this book and reading the synopsis, if it speaks directly to you I encourage you to invest in yourself by purchasing it. What if the breakthrough you are waiting on, is waiting on you to ***BREAK THROUGH!***

Men are not just using condoms

BREAK THROUGH

They are wearing them!

To break out of something; is to break into something!

What are you breaking into that's worth you breaking out?

1

The Story of Judah and Tamar

About this time, Judah left home and moved to Adullam, where he visited a man named Hirah. 2There he met a Canaanite woman, the daughter of Shua, and he married her. 3She became pregnant and had a son, and Judah named the boy Er. 4Then Judah's wife had another son, and she named him Onan. 5And when she had a third son, she named him Shelah. At the time of Shelah's birth, they were living at Kezib. 6When his oldest son, Er, grew up, Judah arranged his marriage to a young woman named Tamar. 7But Er was a wicked man in the Lord's sight, so the Lord took his life. 8Then Judah said to Er's brother Onan "You must marry Tamar, as our law requires of the brother of a man who has died. Her first son from you will be your brother's heir."

Er was a wicked man in the sight of the Lord, so the Lord took his life. This lets me know that we must be concerned about how God views us; not man.

Man of God, are you a wicked man in God's sight?

9But Onan was not willing to have a child who would not be his own heir. So whenever he had intercourse with Tamar he spilled the semen on the ground to keep her from having a baby who would belong to his brother. 10But the Lord considered it to be a wicked thing for Onan to deny a child to his dead brother. So the Lord took Onan's life, too.

Onan was told to go marry Tamar and get her pregnant, giving his brother an heir, which would be the first born son. But Onan disobeyed, by having intercourse with Tamar and spilling the semen on the ground keeping her from getting pregnant, because he refused to give his deceased brother a living heir.

And the Lord considered this to be a wicked thing, for Onan to deny a child to his dead brother. So the Lord took Onan's life too.

Er lost his life because he was wicked and evil. Then, Onan lost his life because he committed wickedness in the sight of God. So Man of God, one brother was evil and the other did evil things. Both killed by God!

Are you doing wicked things or being disobedient in the sight of God?

We all are always concerned about what others will say or how they will look at us, but it's time for us to start being concerned with what the Lord considers evil and how He views us.

11Then Judah told Tamar, his daughter – in – law; not to marry again at the same time but to return to her parents' home. She was to remain a widow until his youngest son, Shelah, was old enough to marry her. But Judah did not really intend to do this because he was afraid Shelah would also die like his two brothers. So Tamar went home to her parents.

Men stop allowing your parents, or shall I say your mother, blame your fiancé/wife for you being dead. She is not the problem! I know you are thinking, "But I am not dead."

Let's get a better understanding of the word dead. Better yet let me define it.

Dead is lacking life. Lacking vitality or brilliance, dispassionate; ancient or out of date: no longer productive or useful; absolute; exhausted.

Er and Onan are both deceased now and still Tamar is not pregnant. She was instructed by Judah (her father – in – law) to go home with her parents and stay a widow until Shelah gets old enough to marry her, knowing he had no intentions on giving his son to her. Because he was afraid he would die as well. But she was unaware so she did as she was told.

Man of God, when is the last time the woman did as you instructed her? You cannot remember can you? Are you following the instructions of Christ?

The deceit started with Judah. Your deception will soon deceive you!

12In the course of time Judah's wife died. After the time of mourning was over, Judah and his friend Hirah the Adullamite went to Timnah to supervise the shearing of his sheep. 13Someone told Tamar that her father – in – law had left for the sheep – shearing at Timnah. 14Tamar was aware that Shelah had grown up. But they had not called her to marry him.

The word gets around!

Tamar was aware that Shelah was old enough to marry, but they had not yet arrange for them to marry.

Say out loud, "Tamar takes matters into her own hands!" You and I both know the worse thing a man can do to a woman, is break his promise to her. And having her wait while making a fool of her! Have you made any promises to the Woman of God that you didn't keep?

So she changed out of her widow's clothing and covered herself with a veil to disguise herself. Then she sat along the road at the entrance to the village of Enaim, which is on the way to Timnah.

Tamar disguised and covered herself with a veil and sat beside the road at the entrance to the village of Enaim, that's on the way to Timnah.

Basically, she set up a plan to deceive Judah. She was in a place that he would pass her by.

15Judah noticed her as he went by and thought she was a prostitute, since her face was veiled. 16So he stopped and propositioned her to sleep with him, not realizing that she was his own daughter – in – law.

He is biting the bait guys! He was unaware of this being his daughter – in - law and propositioned her for sexual relations. His wife was deceased and he was in need of sex.

"How much will you pay me?" Tamar asked. 17"I will send you a young goat from my flock," Judah promised.
"What pledge will you give me so I can be sure you will send it?" she asked.
18"Well what do you want?" he inquired.
She replied, "I want your identification seal, your cord, and the walking stick you are carrying."

Negotiation began.

So Judah gave these items to her. She then let him sleep with her, and she became pregnant. 19Afterwards, she went home, took off her veil, and put on her widow's clothing as usual.

She negotiated with Judah and she got what she requested as collateral. She proceeded to meet his need, after she was secured. Sounds like a business transaction to me.

Man of God, does she feel safe with you? What have you given her to reassure her that you will keep your promise?

Mission accomplished!

20Judah asked his friend Hirah the Adullamite to take the young goat back to her and to pick up the pledges he had given her, but Hirah couldn't find her. 21So he asked the men who lived there, "Where can I find the prostitute who was sitting beside the road at the entrance to the village?"

Judah tried to make good on his promise, by sending his friend to deliver the promise and pick up his pledges. Have you ever sent someone to make good on your promise? Keep your word man of God.

But it's strange how Judah will keep his promise to a stranger, or shall I say a prostitute, but not his daughter – in law. Please make note of this! You cannot choose when you will keep your word, you should always be a man of your word.

His friend Hirah was a true friend because he tried to find her at all cost.

"We've never had a prostitute here." They replied. 22So Hirah returned to Judah and told him that he couldn't find her anywhere and that the men of the village had claimed they didn't have a prostitute there. 23"Then let her keep the pledges!" Judah exclaimed. "We tried our best to send her the goat. We'd be the laughingstock of the village if we went back again."

Judah knew he had a reputation to live up to, like many men today. So he was not willing to jeopardize it. I must admit, he tried to keep his promise.

24About three months later, word reached Judah that Tamar, his daughter – in – law was pregnant as a result of prostitution. "Bring her out and burn her!" Judah shouted. 25But as they were taking her out to kill her, she sent this message to her father – in – law: "The man who owns this identification seal and walking stick is the father of my child. Do you recognize them?"

Okay let's pause for a second.   Three months later, word reached Judah that Tamar was pregnant as a result of prostitution. The word got out often around there!

Judah was furious with Tamar bringing shame on him and his family, by being pregnant as a result of prostitution! He instructed them to bring her out and burn her! Meaning he is going to kill her publicly, in front of everyone!

Man of God, have you been in such rage with your wife that you almost wanted to kill her? Maybe just one thought that you can remember, when you said, "I wish she was dead!" You probably never shared this with anyone but you felt it.

But somehow she had ammunition to fight back!

As they took her out to kill her, she pulled out her ammunition! Her ammunition was what she negotiated three months prior, which was what Judah gave her as collateral, his identification seal and walking stick.

I am sure Tamar was scared to death but she dealt the hand and now she had to play her hand carefully. She had everything to lose and even more to gain. Her life was at risk, along with her unborn child.

Judah do you recognize them?

26Judah admitted that they were his and said, "She is more in the right than I am, because I didn't keep my promise to let her marry my son Shelah." But Judah never slept with Tamar again.

Judah took responsibility of his part and sparred her life. He is an honest man because he told the truth. He openly admitted they belong to him and he accepted that she was pregnant by him. This speaks highly of his character.

I know so many men, who lay with women and get them pregnant but deny the child is his. In most cases even deny he had ever slept with the mother of the child. Man of God, could this be you? She might not be your wife. It could have been an affair, but is it yours? Maybe this could have been when you were a teenager but you denied it.

This is not to judge you but to make you aware of it, giving you a chance to return and take ownership of what and who belongs to you.

27In due season the time of Tamar's delivery arrived, and she had twin sons.

In due season you shall receive double for your trouble! We hear this regularly from pastors, that you will receive double for your trouble. This has just been confirmed.

Tamar was married to two of Judah's sons and she didn't bear a child for either one of them. Then, he denied her his third son. But she was rewarded with two sons. I think she birthed two sons, representing both husbands, through the seeds of their father. Let's not forget this was a blessing to Judah as well.

28As they were being born, one of them reached out his hand, and the midwife tied the scarlet thread around the wrist of the child who appeared first, saying "This one came out first."

29But then he drew back his hand, and the other baby was actually the first to be born.

"What!" the midwife exclaimed. "How did you break out first?" And ever after he was called Perez. 30Then the baby with the scarlet thread on his wrist was born, and he was named Zerah.

One appeared to be delivered first but as he drew his hand back, the other twin son broke through becoming the first born named Perez! *Perez* means *break through* and *Zerah,* the second born, means *arise.*

Now that I have laid the foundation of this message, it is time for me to build the house.

Can I preach this word as if I was standing outside of a liquor store or in the pulpit? It really does not matter to me whether I am on my front porch or standing outside the door of the church.

I have preached this word in the barbershops, on the telephone. Every time I felt the Holy Spirit move over those men and women like no other. I pray the same anointing falls afresh upon you and this word will come alive in you.

Father God, decrease me and increase you! None of me but all of you! God, I ask that your anointing reign down on the man of God, that is reading this book right now in Jesus' Name Amen!

You may be a man that has been told your wife is barren and cannot have children, or you are infertile and cannot produce a child. The doctor gave you this news months or years ago and you believed it.

Though you continue to pray and cry at night begging God to bless her womb, you really do not believe it will happen. Why? Because you have not yet been blessed with a child. Hold your faith and continue to read.

Or maybe you are a man that has a vision to start your own business or ministry, but you have not shared it with her, because you do not believe it will happen. You may not know how to start the business.

Or just maybe you are a man that has closed your heart and though you have a woman or even married, you won't release what's in you into her; so she can birth it out.

Can we just talk one on one? Well, I know you cannot talk back but I want you to relax yourself.

Relax is to ease tension or stress, to be or make less stringent or intense.

You are aware that when reading anything it speaks to where you are, directs you to your next move; gives you clarity and awareness.

But everyone can read the same thing and get something totally different. Why is that? Well, I know of two reasons. One, we have two things that makes us different; our beliefs and experiences.

With those two reasons being brought to the forefront, I ask you, to allow yourself to see this from a different perspective, regardless of our beliefs being different and us having different experiences.

Our experiences and beliefs have such an impact on our lives and the lives of others. We must one day take a look at how they are helping or hurting us.

So let me introduce myself. Hello, I am woman of God after God's own heart. I have been hurt, abandoned, abused mentally, emotionally, and physically by a man I once loved. I was beat with a pistol, spit in my face, and stomped while I was carrying his child. And the year my daughter walked across the stage to get her diploma, he had the audacity to tell me I deserved every bit of it!

I guess, you are questioning what did she do to deserve that? I did not love myself and I allowed him to do everything he did to me.

The reason I am sharing this is because this could have been the very reason I cut men off and decided to never deal with a man again. No, I did not cut them off for life, thank God!

Nevertheless, I did shut them out for six years of my life.

Not to mention, I experienced abandonment first from my father. For years, I was unaware of what abandonment was because I never had him in my everyday life, so it was familiar to me. But I expected something different from him.

Man of God, are you giving the woman of God something different or are you duplicating what he (her father or ex) did? Good or bad?

But should every man pay for what he has done to me? Absolutely not. It is not fair to me or the man that is ordained to be my husband. So I decided to destroy the wall I built, shutting men out not allowing him in, but not allowing me to come out either. Breaking the wall will help me have who God designed for me and for me to do His purpose.

That is why this book has been written. Just as women build walls out of steal and cement and men cannot reach her; men have done the same thing.

Men are not just using condoms; they are wearing them!

Men wear condoms protecting themselves from being hurt, but in reality you are killing yourself. Because the vision that God has placed inside of you, is designed to be released into a woman (your wife), so she can birth it out!

2

The Lessons of Judah

Man of God, the first lesson I want to point out to you is how Judah handled Tamar, (his daughter – in –law) differently from the way he treated the prostitute. But they were the same person. But he noticed her to be a prostitute.

He deceived Tamar by giving her instructions to go home and stay single until he calls for her to marry Shelah.

Does this sound like something your friend has told his woman? I'm sure you have not told a woman to let you get yourself together and then you will return to her. Knowing you had no intentions to return to her, because you do not love her in that way. Does this sound familiar?

Basically, I am trying to relate this to our everyday life situations. I know I've been told that on several occasions. I cannot marry you in this condition, let me save some money and get things in order, but it was all deceit! Stop deceiving women. Stop giving them false hope that you will one day return or send for them.

But can I share a secret with you? Judah was afraid! He deceived her only because he was scared he would lose another son. What are you afraid of losing, that you will lie to protect due to you having an earlier lost?

He mourned for the death of his wife. What loss have you not taken adequate time to mourn? Was it an old relationship, loss of a job, or loss of a love one? We must take time to grieve.

After the time of mourning was over, Judah and his friend went to Timnah to supervise the shearing of his sheep.

Meaning he got back into position! This clearly states he was a business man.

Judah was distracted when he saw Tamar, but I believe with his wife being deceased; he missed her. He was vulnerable and sexually frustrated.

He noticed her, stopped and propositioned her, because he perceived her to be a prostitute.

He noticed her as a prostitute. He recognized her as someone other than herself. Though he thought she was a prostitute, she was Tamar. My perception is he perceived her as a business woman. Imagine it, a prostitute is dress for business, has on the attire that will get his attention, and is ready to fulfill his need for a price.

You do not agree? Let's define *prostitute. A prostitute is one who accepts money or other consideration for sex or other base end. To use or offer for base purposes.*

Business is commerce; the buying and selling of goods and services; one's occupation; any activity or matter for concern.

I can define her as a *salesman. Salesman is the exchange of goods and services for money.*

The point I am making, is he seen her differently. Men, you must view your wife and/or significant other from a different perspective. She is there to serve you and the cost is to *love her as Christ loves the church.* Jesus loves the church so much that He died for it!

Then Judah stopped what he was doing and made her an offer. When is the last time you were heading out with your boys and you noticed her? Yes, she looked nice, smelled good, it made you stop and offer yourself to her.

Afterwards, he answered and made her a promise.

How many times has your wife asked you a question and you ignored her? Walking out telling her that you do not want to talk about it right now and you all should talk later. Never answering her questions, this leaves her room to assume.

Unanswered questions are answered with assumptions!

Judah made Tamar a promise.

Let me explain. *A vow is a solemn promise; an emphatic affirmation. To promise solemnly; to make a solemn promise.*

Solemn is sacred; marked by ceremonial observance, majesty, or power.

Yes, I had to explain that in the fullness, because many dilute the strength of a promise. It's a vow before God. She is not the only one who heard your promise. God did! Your vow to your wife was to be with her until death does you apart. Remember? In sickness and in health, richer or poorer. Just reminding a few that forgot. We must keep our promise! A promise is to be kept; not to be neglected.

He then gave her room to negotiate with him by allowing her to ask him "What pledge will you give me so I can be sure you will send it?"

Wow! How many men hate the thought of being questioned by a woman? You hate it especially when she is asking you to prove yourself. The average man answer to this question would have been, "Why are you questioning me? You do not trust me?" He will end the conversation with, "Forget it! Don't worry about it!" Does this sound familiar to you, Man of God?

A man is not afraid of a woman's question, when he knows he is the answer! – Bishop Bronner.

Yes, you are her answer. If you are the solution to her problem, why are you afraid of her questions? I am trying to help you, that is all.

Stop scratching your head; it's going to be alright. *Because when we know better we do better says Bishop Dale C. Bronner.*

So allow your wife or fiancé to ask you questions, so you can solve her problems and/or know how to direct her to the solution.

Then he went further by allowing her to make her request known. "Well what do you want?" he inquired. She replied, "I want your identification seal, your cord, and the walking stick you are carrying."

Allow me to go deeper please. In the above statement she said, "I want."

To want something is to feel a wish for; to desire; to lack; to request or require. To have need, to be destitute. A lack scarcity; poverty.

My God! I just believe the word of God is not hard if one explains it with simplicity. God want us to get the word because how can we obey the word, if we do not understand it? He said, *"In all your getting get understanding."* So I do my best at explaining the word the way I perceive it, so the other individual on the receiving end can get it.

Then Judah gave it to her.

King did you pay attention to what Tamar requested from him? She requested his state identification, birth certificate, and social security card. Guess what? He gave them to her!

I am sure men are saying, "He is crazy!" But men get this, in reality he is letting her know who he is, where he was from, who he was connected to and what he is about. Do you not think this is valuable information that needs to be exchanged between the two, before having sex?

This is something to think about, how many women have you laid with that neither one of you knew anything about each other?

Many men are takers and they are not willing to give. What do you have to contribute to your wife? Can you impart something inside of her that is life changing? Are you able to yield your vision or dream God has placed into you, inside of her?

The thought of your vision gives you a headache, because you cannot bring it forth. It has bothered you for years now! Is the pressure so heavy that you feel you are about to bust? Yes, I am speaking to you Man of God!

After Judah gave Tamar what she requested, she then let him release the pressure. Yes, she liberated him (set him free)!

She let him sleep with her, and she became pregnant.

I know you are sick and tired of fighting her for sex! And tired of having to threaten her with you are going to take it. Would it be nice for a change, for her to willingly serve you?

When a man gets a woman pregnant, she begins to expect something and in her expectancy she starts working towards it. You see how your vision was transferred into her and now she is working on the assignment that was assigned through you.

Yes, she is carrying your seed/vision. She begins to think of names depending on the sex of the child. Then, she starts picking out colors of paint for the bedroom, layaway clothes, pampers, stroller, crib, and walker. She picks out the space that she want to place the crib because what's in you is designed to be conceived, nurtured, and delivered through her.

This is your business I am speaking of! She ponders on names for the business, the best location, and begins picking out the furniture and the accessories.

My God it's powerful!

Judah asked Hirah the Adullamite to take the young goat back to her and pick up the pledges he had given her, but Hirah couldn't find her.

Man of God, this confirms that Judah was trying to make good on the vow he made to her. You made a vow; keep it!

But Hirah couldn't find her anywhere. But remember that no one saw her but Judah. Only you should notice your Queen!

So Hirah returned to Judah with word that he could not find her, and the men at the village claimed they had no prostitute there. Judah instructed Hirah not to go back because they would become the laughingstock. "'Let her keep the pledges!" Judah exclaimed.

I understand how he felt because he tried to keep his word. And she had valuables that belong to him. But he knew his reputation was even more valuable and he could not risk it.

So he cried to God! Have you cried out to God lately? Are you aware that crying out to God is a way of communicating with Him? He knows what every tear represents.

I do not think I have to say much about reputation. This clearly defines that you will be inspected by your fruit. Your actions toward others will define who you are. If you are not a liar; do not lie. If you are a man of your word, it will show.

Opinions of others, concerning you, does matter. Because they share their opinions with others!

Never give anyone a reason to say anything bad about you if you can help it.

About three months later, word reached Judah that Tamar, his daughter – in – law, was pregnant as a result of prostitution. "Bring her out and burn her!" Judah shouted.

Judah was so upset. I mean, he had lost two sons, then his wife, and was reluctant to get his pledges back. It was one thing after another and now he is hearing that his daughter – in – law is pregnant! She has brought embarrassment upon his family and him. "Kill her!" Judah says.

But as they were taking her out to kill her, she sent this message to her father – in – law: "The man who owns this identification seal and walking stick is the father of my child. Do you recognize them?" All I can say is, "He just received the pregnancy results, with his DNA all over it!"

He admitted that they were his and said, "She is more in the right than I am, because I did not keep my promise to let her marry my son Shelah." But Judah never slept with Tamar again.

These are my confessions! I am sorry, I thought for a moment I heard the sound of Usher singing in the background.

Judah confessed that the items belonged to him, but in that statement he acknowledged that the children belonged to him too. He also validated that he did not keep his promise to her.

This is letting you know that even when you do wrong, still be a man and own up to it.

But he never slept with her again. Well, she tricked him once, but he made it known he was not going to be deceived again.

In due season, the time of Tamar's delivery arrived, and she had two sons.

Do you see the blessing in this? You do remember he lost two sons? Now God has blessed him with a set of twin sons. This is a great time for you to high five God! Yes, because He allowed the man of God to get a free throw, scoring two extra points because someone fouled him!

Though God took his sons; he blessed him with two more! God can replace anything he takes away.

What the enemy meant for his bad, God turned it around for his good! Look at how Judah was telling them to burn her to death (this was before her due season) not knowing she was pregnant with his two sons. The enemy wanted that death to take place because he would have killed her and his two sons. My God! But God! I sure hope you are getting this!

Earlier we defined the word dead. But now let's define *death. Death is the termination of life.*

Now do you see that there's a difference in being dead and being put to death. We may experience being dead but God can bring us back to life.

The enemy wants to call death upon you! But no weapon formed shall prosper. Your vision shall come fourth, In Jesus' Name!

As they were being born, one of them reached out his hand, and the midwife tied the scarlet thread around the wrist of the child who appeared first. She said, "This one came out first." But then he drew back his hand, and the other baby was first to be born.

"What!" The midwife exclaimed. "How did you break out first?" And ever after, they called him Perez. Then the baby with the scarlet thread on his wrist came out, and he was named Zerah.

Man of God, I came to speak to the Perez in you. Perez come forth in the mighty name of Jesus! The little boy in you will no longer allow you to stay locked up in bondage. He has busted through the condom, no longer waiting on his breakthrough but he has broken through in Jesus' Name!

Yes, your mother may have hurt you or your father abandoned or rejected you. But today the boy will birth out the Man that lives in you in Jesus' Name!

3

The Twelve Steps of Judah

Judah's twelve steps goes as follows:

1. He mourned.
2. He supervised.
3. He noticed her.
4. He stopped and propositioned her.
5. He answered her.
6. He made her a promise.
7. He was questioned by her.
8. He heard her request.
9. He gave her what she requested.
10. He was liberated through her.
11. He got her pregnant.
12. He admitted they were his.

I once heard TD Jakes say that women talk in circles, but men like to get straight to the point. So let me follow the instructions of a man when dealing with a man.

The one thing people appreciate are those they can relate to or that can relate to them. Otherwise it's really no use. I pray you are relating to what I am sharing In Jesus' Name!

We have scratched the surfaced on the above steps, but let's get more in depth.

As I mentioned earlier you must take time out to mourn over your loss. Mourning is a healing process and it can be longer or shorter, depending on how great the loss was. And it depends on the individual that is mourning.

Grieving an ex is just like experiencing the death of a love one. Many do not know the process is pretty much the same. But the most important thing is that we must go through to get passed it.

I know they say men are not supposed to cry, really? Well, I would not care if you had to cry alone. You better cry, because that helps you heal.

Let me share a personal testimony with you that you may be able to relate to. It's not mine but I am sure he would not mind me sharing.

I can remember my brother being incarcerated while our mother went on to glory. This was a very tough time for him, but he tried to hold it all together. He began reassuring himself and others he is okay but deep down he was lost, broken, scared, and angry!

He eventually got out of jail and my mother left him beneficiary over her life insurance policy. So when he got out of jail he was spending money frivolously, going to the clubs, drinking, smoking, and drugging.

After three months, he was locked back up. Got back out and went back again. But one day he and I were talking and he said, "Kisha you know what I realized?" I said, "What?" He responded, "I never had time to grieve my mother's death. I had to save face to a certain extent in jail because I could not let men think I was weak. Then when I returned home, I medicated it with fame. But my last time around, after taking my counseling sessions seriously, I knew it was time for me to mourn the death of my mother. If not, I would continue to go down this same road that I want to avoid."

Man of God, now do you see the importance of mourning your loss? Today my brother no longer gets high, and is in his children lives, has his own apartment, and keeps a job. He has accepted that our mother is gone but she will forever be in his heart.

I have a similar story myself. It took me ten years to get over my ex fiancé because after dealing with other guys and realizing he was the best thing I've had, I felt guilt for years. It's probably one of the reasons that a few of the relationships after him, did not work out.

I was mourning over him but he had gone on with his life! I begged, stalked, and chased him for years but he grieved his loss but I had not.

King, mourning is necessary, but afterwards you must return to work.

After you have healed from the loss, it's time for you to go back to work. *If a man doesn't work, a man doesn't eat!* Your first work is your household!

People are still under your supervision, so you must return to supervise what you have been entrusted with. God said that He would not put more on you, than you can handle. You can do it!

What is it that God have given you the authority to supervise? Are you doing a good job? Are you loyal?

You may be saying, you're not a manager. Sometime people underestimate themselves because they do not have the title, but do not confuse the title with the position. Let me show you something.

You may be a man that is still at home with your mother, but you're working and helping her. You are contributing to bills, cutting the grass, taking out the trash, etc. Don't down play that of which God gave you control of, because He will judge to see if you were a good steward over it.

Remember the parables of three servants; it's a perfect illustration of being a good servant. Man of God please read **Matthew 25:14-30** this will bless you.

But God also said, "He won't put more on you than you can bear, so know whatever you are faced with, God created you with that particular opposition in mind.

Sometimes managing is not necessarily managing others but it's managing a position. You must manage the position before you are given the title!

My daughter works at Red Lobster. She started working there when she was sixteen and she is now twenty one. She started off as a hostess, and then she got cross-trained for two other positions. She took a year off when she was around twenty, but returned at twenty one and now she is at a new location. I know you are wondering why I am sharing this. Well, let me explain.

She went back as a hostess but then she trained in takeout. Takeout consists of her to act as a manager at the end of the shift, counting every dollar that's made and making sure everything calculates correctly. She is doing the job of a manager but she does not have the title.

Are you in a management position without the title? Many managers have the title but they do not know the job. I would rather do the job and work the position because I can get the title at another location.

In other words, God can be training you in the position for the title to come later on in your life. But He wants to see will you be faithful over the few, so He can bless you with much!

Are you faithful over the Queen he has placed in your life; because she too must be managed properly?

I understand you are a hard worker, but every now and then you must notice your Queen! Have you recognized something different about her lately? No. Well look again.

Did she wash the clothes, clean up, and/or cook lately? Is her hair different? Has she purchased a new perfume? Man of God, have she been in the mood more lately? Yes, the mood. I am trying to give you a hint that it's time for you to notice her! Is she smiling at you more? There's nothing like letting a woman know that you see something different about her.

If you have realized something different about the Woman of God, take time, pause, and approach her. Yes, compliment her by asking her for something that you need. Women love to feel needed. If God made a woman a man's helpmeet, do you think it would be a turn off for you to need her? Not by any means! Examine that word carefully, helpmeet. She was designed to help you by meeting you half way.

Now that was some good teaching. There are too many women out here that has mistaken help for doing it all. No, that is not the way God set it up. The woman is an addition to a man.

Addition: the act or process of adding or uniting.

Proverbs 31:11-12 reads.
11Her husband can trust her, and she will greatly enrich his life.
12She will not hinder him but help him all her life.

A man could come behind his woman and hold her. Saying, "Baby you smell real good. Can you meet me in our bedroom tonight in your birthday suit?" That indirectly tells her she has it! But beware, because now that she knows you are enticed by her newness, she will want something in return.

I am trying to give you the goodies so that you won't come empty handed. Pay attention because this is good information.

Think of it like this, a man hates every time a woman comes to him with her hand out. But women hates the times when a man comes to her with his hand is empty.

What is in your hand? Can she get a massage with your hands? Can you lift her up with your hands? Can you embrace her with your hands?

What am I saying? Meet her halfway. Be willing to give more; to get more because God said, *"To the measure that you give is to the measure you will receive."*

You should not be willing to ask for anything you are not willing to give. But the thing I must share with you Man of God is that women do not want what men want. Our wants are different. Make note of that.

He noticed her, stopped, and propositioned her! Can I put this in my own words? He saw her differently, which got his attention. Then he offered her something, because he had his need in mind. Do you have a considerable offering to get your need met? Do not go empty handed Man of God!

I am helping somebody today! I am in my zone because I was created to help others. I can recall Bishop Bronner saying, "How can you put fish on dry land and expect the fish to swim? Try putting the fish in water and watch the fish swim because it is in its element." That was free so use it wisely.

Are you in your element Man of God? What is it that you do well? Do you love, serve, encourage, support, and/or give, and protect well? If you are not in your element, you are out of position. Being in your element is being in the right position and operating effectively in it.

Speaking of effect, do you communicate effectively with the woman of God? Some men may be asking, "Why does she keeps relating to her as the woman of God. My girl will not even attend church." But she is still a woman of God, as I address you as a man of God. Stay with me because I am trying to make a point.

There is an animal in every woman and man, that brings out animalistic behavior but there is also a King and Queen too. There is the Woman and Man of God as well. So who are you communicating with, in her?

Did the Queen ask you a question but you answered the dog? Did the Woman of God speak to the King but the dog responded? I was just working myself up to the next point.

The next point I would like to make is to please have an answer for the questions she asks and make sure you speak to the appropriate one that is asking the question. Dogs do not understand English and humans cannot speak the language of a dog. Are you with me? Okay let me give you an example.

Have you ever been playing with your wife but she was not in a playful mood? You're playing but she is serious. She begins saying that you are so childish! Now you are offended because all you were doing was playing, so now the heat is on and you both have attitudes for days. Are you aware of what really took place?

What happened was the child was at play and the woman was at work! Women do not take children to work with them. So you must know when and how to invite the girl to the playground with the boy. It's a child in all of us, but we have to play together. Are you feeling me right now?

Man of God, it's okay to enjoy life, take your suit off, kick your feet up and relax, but invite your woman to join you. Remember, be prepared to answer her questions and it will help if you keep your need in mind.

Have you ever had a promise made to you and someone broke it? How is a promise broken? Can I answer that? By not fulfilling it! A made promise should be a paid promise!

To pay is to give something of value in return for goods or services; to reward or punish: to render, as a compliment. To make payment; to be profitable. Compensation.

Man of God, can I speak to the son in you? The son that was told daddy will be back to take you school shopping, but he never returned. Whose mother said that she was going to buy those shoes for you tomorrow, but you have yet worn them.

Now read the above definition again. Do you see where it clearly states to pay is to reward or punish. If a person fails to keep their promise to another, the other person is now being punished for them breaking their promise!

Not to mention, Man of God (yes now I am talking back to the man) when that was done to you as a child, you grew up to be a man. The woman makes the man a promise but fails to render it. The boy begins to communicate with the man saying, "See, she is just like your mother and father!"

We have all been made promises, and received promises, some kept and some were broken. But moving forward, be sure you can keep your promise because where there is a broken promise; there's a broken heart! Can you relate?

Have you had a sit down with your Queen lately? No. Why not? Could it be because every time the both of you talk she starts asking all kinds of questions, that you have no idea where they are even coming from. Yes, I understand. I wish you could see my face right now with this "Kool-Aid" smile on it!

I am laughing out loud because I have a seventeen year young son that looks at me strangely when out of nowhere I ask him questions? He has even asked me, "Mama where did that come from?" But I want to soothe your anxieties, do not be afraid of our questions!

It's just a question; which needs an answer. I have a friend that once shared with me that questions that are asked does not always have an answer at that time. So in other words, think about it before answering it. By simply saying, "That's a good question. Let me get back with you." But please do just that and get back with her, with an answer.

We as women are more concerned when men do not answer the question. Sometimes certain questions pop up in our heads because we are thinkers. Some people are over thinkers; such as me. At times I do not know where it comes from or why? I do not have an answer for myself. So I ask someone else, because just maybe they can help me figure it out. But let me tell you a secret, every question a woman asks, is not about you!

A man afraid of a woman's questions; does not have answers to his own. Start answering those questions in your head or ask her so she can do her job, by helping you figure it out. This is just my insight on it. I am laughing out loud because now I know I have you pondering on everything I said; or maybe not. Just know she will have questions that only the Man of God and King can answer!

The next time your wife calls out your name, your response should be, "What do you need?" That is giving her a chance to petition you for something, but you are letting her know upfront you can deliver it.

Years ago, I worked as a receptionist and I remember being taught to answer the phone. I would say, 'Thank you for calling Outreach, Shakisha speaking I can help." I was answering the call letting the individual know that I was capable of meeting their need.

When the woman of God makes her request known, be sure to satisfy it!

Whatever you do, do not close this book right now! This is where you have been trying to get to all of this time without even knowing it.

I am about to ask you to allow your imagination to run wild. Yes, I am giving you permission to go there. Do you have an imagination? Do you allow it to visit places you have never been? Well, come go with me. Where to? Jail!

Imagine yourself being arrested. But the strange thing about this arrest, you have handcuffed yourself. Now who will do such a thing? You will.

Go purchase a condom or go get the one out of your wallet. You know that's not where you are supposed to keep them right? Condoms are supposed to be kept in a cool dry place. Like the refrigerator. Why? So they won't break! You are trying to protect yourself, right?

I hope you did not go get the condom for real. I said, "Turn on your imagination." I will be sure to tell you when to turn it off. I promise.

At the very end of this book I defined some words, one of them is condom. *A condom is thin rubber sheath worn on a man's penis during sexual intercourse as a contraceptive and/or as protection against infection.*

Can I please break the above paragraph down so that you can get a full understanding of what I am saying? I have specific words underlined, that I felt was relevant for this teaching. Read the following definitions.

Sheath is to place or enclose in or as in a sheath or covering.

Sheathe is to put into a sheath; to protect or conceal, as by covering.

Worn is frayed, damaged, etc. by wear; showing the effects of worry, anxiety, etc. Hackneyed.

Penis is the male genital organ of higher vertebrates, carrying the duct for the transfer of sperm during copulation.

Sexual intercourse is sexual contact between individuals involving penetration, esp. the insertion of a man's erect penis into a woman's vagina, typically culminating in orgasm and the ejaculation of semen.

Contraceptive is capable of preventing conception.

Protection is the safeguard against damage or harm. The action of protecting someone or something, or the state of being protected.

Yes, I guess you can call this sex one on one. But seriously, I am trying to really get my point across. Does it take for us to define every word to get it? Maybe it does.

Come on let's get it!

Visualize you putting on that thin rubber sheath, around your penis before having sexual intercourse with your wife, because you are using a contraceptive to protect yourself.

You have concealed your penis, not allowing the transfer of your sperm, to flow from you into her during copulation. *Copulation simply means sexual intercourse.*

So you are wearing a form of contraceptive to stop the conception. *Conception is a beginning, an impression or understanding. To conceive is to imagine and/or understand.*

And you thought your wife was barren!

Can we please define one more vital word of importance? Thank you, because this will bring it home.

Vagina – (From Latin vagina, literally "__sheath__" is fibro muscular elastic tubular tract which is a sex organ and has two main functions: SEXUAL INTERCOURSE AND CHILD BIRTH! In humans, this passage leads from the opening of the uterus (womb), but the vaginal tract at the cervix. Unlike men who have one genital orifice, women have two, the urethra and the vagina. The vaginal opening is much larger than the urethral opening, and both openings are protected by the labia. The inner mould of the vagina has a fold, which can create FRICTION for the penis DURING INTERCOURSE. During AROUSAL, the vagina gets MOIST to FACILITATE the ENTRANCE of the PENIS.

Wow! That's all I can say.

Man of God, as I was reading the above definition of vagina the first word that stood out to me was *SHEATH*! Could it be that you are protecting yourself from the protector? God designed the woman to help a man; not hurt him.

Then it clearly stated that a female sex organ is for two main functions sexual intercourse and childbirth, which immediately took me back to when Onan was told to marry Tamar and get her pregnant! But what did he do? During sexual intercourse, he spilled the semen on the ground. God seen this as a wicked thing and killed him!

I also noticed it does not say Onan spilled "*his* semen", it says "*the* semen". So could this semen belong to God? Yes, the Creator of all.

Also it says the inner mould of the vagina has a fold, which can create friction for the penis during sexual intercourse and during arousal. The vagina gets moist to facilitate the entrance of the penis.

Man of God, do you see how even a woman's body was designed to take care of you. God has a built a fold inside of a woman so it can rub you down. And during arousal she moistens to make it easy for you to enter.

I hope and pray that you snatch that condom off of your heart, body, and soul. And begin foreplay with her thoughts to get her aroused. Allow her to moisten, so you can have an easy entrance, in order to deliver your vision. That she may conceive it, nurture it, and bring it forth. But during the process of conception, you will no longer remain in your imaginative state because at this moment I am calling you out.

You can stop imagining your Gift being birth, but go give birth to it! Because this is the only way the Queen can *LIBERATE* the King!

As the King is set free, the Queen will get pregnant and I am sure after all of this teaching you will not have a problem with admitting that it is YOURS!

4

The Teachings of Tamar

Man of God, you are aware that you can learn things from a woman, right? I remember speaking at a men's group home, my very first time, sharing my testimony with a group men. I really did not think I had much to say that would interest a man.
But God placed something on my heart!

After talking two hours straight to ten men that had just finished working a twelve hour shift, neither one of them nodded or looked away from me. This man stood up before I left and said, "Ms. Lady, I am sixty five years young. I have never listened to a woman not even my mother, because I felt a woman could not tell me anything. But after listening to you tonight, I have a lot of women to call and make amends with. You are the first woman that ever said anything that made me take a look at myself, and I thank you."

I must say that is when I knew I was on the right path. All ten of those men embraced me and said, "Please continue to do what you are doing!"

I am not sure if you feel the same way he felt but I hope that after you read this portion of the book, it will change your perspective as well.

Tamar's lessons goes as follows:

1. She obeyed him.
2. She disguised herself.
3. She wore a veil.
4. She waited for him.
5. She questioned him.
6. She made him comfortable.
7. She negotiated with him.
8. She collected the collaterals from him.
9. She secured the deal with him.
10. She let him sleep with her.
11. The purpose was fulfilled for both of them.
12. Mission was accomplished.

Man of God, I bet you money after reading the above lessons of Tamar, you would love for your wife to do the same thing. Well, if you paid attention to Judah's teaching, you may be able to get her to do just that.

She obeyed because she wasn't aware that she was being deceived by him, so I believe she trusted him.

When trust is broken it is much harder to get her to trust you again. Please make sure she can trust you. Trust is earned, yet given freely in the beginning of a relationship. If no one gives you a reason not to trust them, there is no reason not to. The moment it is taken away, to earn it back can be the most difficult thing to do. Please build her confidence in you and make sure you continue maintaining it.

As I mentioned to the woman of God, a man does not want to see the same thing all the time. Men are visual and you must do whatever it takes to get his attention and keep it.

But Man of God, you must change up a little every now and then too. We love our man but we love to smell some nice cologne, to see him with a fresh haircut and shave, and new gear. I mean spice it some! You did it when you first met her, right? You know they say that you must do what you did to get her in order to keep her.

Are you a man that is on fire for God? Do you always beat her up with the word? Every time the woman of God speaks with you, she does not want to hear the word of God. Sometimes she just wants to have a regular conversation. I am not saying do not love God and serve him with all you have. All I am saying is balance your conversations with her.

Do not make her feel intimidated by you, because you know more scriptures than she. The word says... *study to show yourself approve.* So show her with your actions.

If you feel she is not knowledgeable of something, take time and study the word with her. *Iron sharpens iron.* Men should want their woman sharp!

Tamar waited on Judah and she did not wait long. King do not leave your Queen waiting on you! Women dislike when a man tells her to be ready at a certain time and he shows up late, never calling to say he is in traffic or running behind schedule. Please value her time because time is valuable and we should not waste it. I am sure you would not like it if a woman kept you waiting either.

We have already discussed the importance of a woman being able to ask questions, I know you got this.

But for the record King, if you have questions you better ask them too. I may have already said that, I am sure I did.

But an individual cannot blame you for not knowing the answer to something they never asked.

I shared earlier that Tamar can teach you something, I hope she is doing exactly that. Can I flip the table around though?

Below I have listed a few questions for you to answer.

1. How comfortable are you with your wife?
2. Can you tell her practically anything even if it will hurt her?
3. Do you feel she can tell you anything regardless of what it is?
4. Do you all have room to bargain with one another? Or is everything your way or her way?
5. Does she have proof that you are a good or bad man (to her)?
6. Is she safe with you or scared of you? A woman that is afraid of you is not doing what you say because she wants to, but because she is made to.
7. Do you feel empowered by forcing her to do what you say or when she willingly does what she is told?
8. Does she let you sleep with her? Does she come on to you? Does she turn you on?
9. Do you have unfulfilled needs?
10. Does she have requested wants unfulfilled?

A woman that does not live in fear will always be sincere.

If you give her what she wants, there is a guarantee you will get what you need. But I believe everyone deserves a fresh start by starting fresh.

Do you want a fresh start? Are willing to give her one? If so, proceed.

If the woman of God has a debt owed to you, will you charge it off and allow her to start fresh by erasing every bad memory of hurt and/or anger?

Yes. Great! You are on your way to master the teachings of *BREAK THROUGH!*

I hope that you have collected the value of this word, that's now secure within, to let the purpose of God flow through you, and allow her to become pregnant with your vision. In order to complete His mission!

5

A Word from the Lord

God has purposed you for purpose. He made you in his image and His likeness. He made you master over all life – the fish in the sea, the birds in the sky, and all the livestock, wild animals, and small animals. He formed your body from the dust of the ground and breathed into it the breath of life. And you became a living person. He noticed that it was not good for man to be alone and realized that it was not anything suitable for you. God said, "I will make a companion who will help him." So He caused you to fall into a deep sleep, He took one of your ribs; created a woman. He brought her to you and you shouted, "At last!" "She is part of my own flesh and bone! She will be called woman because she was taken out of man." This explains why a man leaves his father and mother and is joined to his wife, and the two are united into one.

I know this is what Adam said but man of God you must own this now!

You will no longer wait for a breakthrough; you will *break through*!

Imagine another man having you in the headlock, what are you going to do?

Need I say more? In this hour at this time I pray that the word take root and bare much fruit in your life, In Jesus' Name!

It's not over until God says it's over. But guess what, it has actually just begun!

The year of 2014, is a year of abundance! This is your year to *BREAK THROUGH!* God said, *"We are to have life and have it more abundantly!"*

Abundant: Plentiful. Bountiful. More than enough!

Man of God, this is so powerful! Please open up your spiritual ears that you may hear the Lord speak directly to you right in this hour, this is God!

God said, "I will make a companion who will help him." He made a woman, from the rib of a man and then allowed the man to name her. But the most important word that describes your fiancé and/or wife is *your helper.*

Do you see how God allowed the deception of Tamar which started with Judah end up blessing Judah? Had Tamar not deceived him, he would have never gotten the blessing of the two sons. God took two sons from him due to their wickedness, but He gave him back a set of twin sons.

What God takes; He can replace!

The word says, *"God knows the heart of a man."*

I believe that God knew Judah was a good man with a good heart, but he was afraid to give his last son to Tamar. Also, Tamar was not trying to hurt Judah but she wanted what belonged to her. So God looked past their deception and brought forth His blessing!

6

In My Own Words

Can I talk with my homie? Check this is out. I know you should have it by now. Did I at least wake up the dream in you? I am sure you have it, but in building anything you must first lay the foundation. Then proceed to build the house, put the pipes and the electrical outlets in, and etc. The most important part I enjoy is decorating it. You know women love to put their final touch on it. So may I have your permission to put the final touch to this?

Er was a wicked man, Onan did a wicked thing in God's sight and the Lord took their lives.

Who are you and what are you doing in God's sight?

Will it put you to death?

Tamar was told to return home to her parents, remain a widow, and he will send for her when his son is old enough to marry. But he knew that was not what he intended to do.

This is when the deception began. He deceived her first. Who have you lied to?

Then Tamar got word!

She then took off the old garments and put on the new. She dressed for the occasion; it was time to handle her business.

She went and waited, but she knew two things that were working in her favor. One, he was sexually frustrated due to his wife being deceased. Two, she was looking too good, for him not to notice her.

Right timing. Timing is everything!

Judah noticed her, stopped, and propositioned her.

She appeared to be a prostitute in his sight. Meaning his vision was not clear. But she did not go off on him when he offered her money for sex. One, she knew she was not a prostitute. Two, she knew it was a gift in him to make boys because he once had three sons.

She knew it was purpose in him that needed to be transferred into her. Guess what? It was more valuable than who he thought she was.

She was not a bit bothered about how he viewed her outer appearance because she was more concerned about his inner appearance (potential).

But she needed collateral to keep herself alive. Sometimes we know if we get caught, we can get a life sentenced or the death penalty. But if we have a witness or some form of proof, it might get thrown out.

She needed proof.

She did not care about the initial promise (the young goat), that was just a part of the negotiation. Sometimes when signing an agreement, there are things in the contract that really does not matter.

Have you ever made a deal with someone and they gave you something extra for free if you joined that day, but really you had no use of it. Tamar did not want a goat. She needed proof that they had slept together, because she knew she was fertile. It was her time of ovulation and tonight she was planning on conceiving a child by Judah!

It reminds me of when Ruth went and laid at Boaz's feet. Naomi said, *"Don't worry daughter, he will make good on this tonight!"*

Tamar knew tonight I am getting pregnant with his vision and I am going to need the DNA results before my delivery, so he can spare my life!

After she negotiated, reached an agreement, and requested what she wanted; he then gave it to her. Consequently she let him sleep with her. Not fighting him off saying, "I am tired. Not tonight. Never mind, maybe next time."

She gave of herself so she could receive the purpose that was in him.

Give and it shall be given. To the measure you give is the measure you shall receive.

Man of God TONIGHT you will *BREAK THROUGH!*

Are you excited?

Do you realize Tamar talked to no one about anything? Man of God, listen to me. Talk to no one about anything, but go before God right now trusting and believing that whatever you desire to bring forth in this Season; tonight is the night!

This may be your night for you to write your vision, share your mission, and/or become fertile. But tonight this word is preparing you to open yourself to release the anointing of the Holy Spirit, to birth what was once called potential!

After Tamar got pregnant, she went home and went to business as usual.

About three months later, Judah got word that Tamar was pregnant as a result of handling her business.

Say out loud, in three months, she will be pregnant with my Gift, as a result of handling her business!

Are you afraid? Because you feel you all cannot afford another child or a child at all. Are you wondering how? You have tried for years and now of all times. You are not able to leave your job and start a business! Or are you starting a ministry? How can you all work and do ministry fulltime?

Fear not, because you can do this. There is no turning back now! Be prepared because she has her sword (ammunition)!

Look at the vision and say, "Yes, this belongs to me; it's mine! I admit, I shared my vision with her and she ran with the vision!"

In due season, the opening day will give birth not to just one but two! God will give you back what you lost but he will give her double the trouble. *"So get ready, get ready, get ready!"- TD Jakes.*

"The time to be ready; is not the time to get ready!" - Bishop Dale C. Bronner.

As Tamar was giving birth, the midwife put the scarlet onto, what appeared to be, the first born son's wrist.

But the second child, named Perez came first, BREAKING THROUGH!

In order for the midwife to have the scarlet prepared to be put on the first born, they had to have known it was two before her delivery date. Someone did an ultrasound!

The ultrasound read, "Man of God, my son I have blessed your wife's womb to give birth to two sons!"

As a result of it, in due season she shall bring forth two ministries, two businesses, and/or two children. One named *BREAK THROUGH* and the other named *ARISE!*

THIS IS YOUR *BREAK THROUGH* SEASON AND YOU SHALL *ARISE* NOW IN JESUS' NAME!

Let this word be a penetration to your heart and allow God to put His Super to your natural, causing a Supernatural Blessing to override your deception and bringing forth the Blessing of God!

The potential gift, when birthed out, becomes the blessing of God.

While studying the word potential, I realized the first six letters reads potent.

Potent is having great power, influence, or effect.

Potent is Powerful, Strong, Mighty, formidable, influential, dominant, and forceful.

I pray the potency of this message, revive and revolutionize your very being that you spring forth into your prosperity in Jesus' Name.

7

Scriptures Just For You

Romans 12:15
When others are happy, be happy with them. If they are sad, share their sorrow.

Matthew 25:20 – 21
The servant to whom he had entrusted the five bags of gold said, "Sir, you gave me two bags of gold to invest, and I doubled the amount." The master was full of praise. "Well done my good and faithful servant. You have been faithful in handling this small amount, so now I will give you many more responsibilities. Let's celebrate together!"

Genesis 2:18
And the Lord God said, "It is not good for the man to be alone. I will make him a companion who will help him."

Romans 2:1
And so, dear brothers and sisters,* I plead with you to give your bodies to God. Let them be a living and holy sacrifice – the kind he will accept. When you think of what he has done for you, is this too much to ask for?

Proverbs 15:1
A gentle answer turns away wrath, but harsh words stir up anger.

Philippians 4:19
And this same God who takes care of me will supply all your needs from his glorious riches, which have been given to us in Christ Jesus.

Matthew 7:7 - 8
Keep on asking, and you will be given what you ask for. Keep on looking, and you will find. Keep on knocking, and the door will be open. 8For everyone who asks, receives. Everyone who seeks, finds. And the door is opened to everyone who knocks.

Philippians 4:6
Don't worry about anything; instead, pray about everything. Tell God what you need, and thank him for all he has done.

Luke 6:38
If you give, you will receive. Your gift will return to you in full measure, pressed down, shaken together to make room, and running over. Whatever measure you use in giving – large or small – it will be used to measure what is given back to you.

John 8:36
So if the Son sets you free, you will indeed be free.

Habakkuk 2:2

Then the Lord said to me, "Write my answer in large, clear letters on a tablet, so that a runner can read it and tell everyone else. But the things I plan won't happen right away. Slowly steadily, surely, the time approaches when the vision will be fulfilled. If it seems slow, wait patiently, for it will surely take place. It will not be delayed.

James 5:16

Confess your sins to each other and pray for each other so that you may be healed. The earnest prayer of the righteous person has great power and wonderful results.

Below are definitions of words that are discussed during the seven chapters of this book. Read and study them.

Wicked is evil, mischievous, or roguish; mean or troublesome.

Breakthrough is an important finding.

Break is to fracture, split and rupture.

Break is to breach or fracture, a stopping or pause, a sudden move, to split, come apart, to become inoperable, to sever relationships, to appear or happen suddenly, to run away, to part by force, to ruin or cause to fail, to violate the terms of a contract.

Through is to complete, done and finish.

Condoms is a thin rubber sheath worn on a man's penis during sexual intercourse as a contraceptive and/or as protection against infection. The deliberate use of artificial methods or other techniques to prevent pregnancy as a consequence of sexual intercourse.

Use is the act of using or the state of being used. The purpose for which something is used.

Wear is to have on the person, as a garment or ornament; to display, as an aspect; to damage by constant use, to exhaust. To be diminished by use, to withstand the effects of use, time, etc. To have a tiring effect. The act of wearing or being worn; articles of dress, destruction from use or time, durability.

Deceived is to mislead as by lying or trickery. To practice deceit.

Afraid is filled with fear or apprehension. Anxious about something.

Lose is to be deprived of, as through carelessness, theft, or legal action; unable to keep: to rid oneself of. To endure loss.

Mourn is to express grief or sorrow.

Supervise is to have charge of. To oversee or manage.

Notice is an announcement or warning; observation or attention. To observe or become aware of.

Stop is to bring to a halt; to prevent the completion of; to withhold or cut off; to cease doing; to check or stanch; to fill in or close as with a cork. To come to a halt. The act of stopping; an obstruction.

Proposition is something offered for consideration.

Answer is any response to a question, inquiry or request; an action in kind: retaliation. The solution to a problem. To respond or reply; to prove sufficient to. To be accountable. To correspond. To speak, write or act in response; to be sufficient; to correspond.

Promise is to pledge or vow.

Solemn is sacred; marked by ceremonial observance, majesty, or power.

Questioned is an inquiry; something open to discussion.   To interrogate; to doubt; to challenge. To ask.

Request is something asked for or to express a desire.

Give is to contribute, impart; to yield to pressure.

Liberate is to set free, as from bondage or onerous convention.

Onerous is difficult or troublesome.

Pregnant is carrying a developing offspring; significant or meaningful.

Expecting is to anticipate as likely or deserving.

Instruct is to educate or edify; to order or direct firmly. To discharge the duties of an instructor.

Exclaim is to cry out suddenly.

Reputation is the way in which one is regarded by others.

Admit is to accept as valid; confessed; acclaimed; acknowledged.

Potential is having the capacity to become or develop into something in the future.

Birth is the emergence of a baby or other young from the body of its mother; the start of life as a physical separate being.

Blessing is God's favor and protection.

Potent means having great power, influence or effect.

Potent is Powerful, Strong, Mighty, formidable, influential, dominant, and forceful.

Everything has meaning. Below are very important characters that are discussed and the meaning of their names.

Tamar means 'date palm tree'.

Judah means 'give praise to God'.

Er spelt backwards in Hebrew is the word evil.

Onan means 'the virile one'.

Zerah means arise.

Perez means he who pushes through. The one who breaks through a wall.

Kezib is a place in the plain of Judah.

Your breakthrough is through her! Your vision is her mission!

For that reason, I need you to see and treat yourself differently. Then she will do the same.

"People do not treat you the way you treat them; they treat you the way you treat yourself." - Shakisha Edness.

Now it's time for you to labor in Prayer, Praise, and Worship; as if you know God is about to bless through you, In Jesus' Name!

Loose your Vision, Ministry, and Business into her NOW!

ABOUT THE AUTHOR

SHAKISHA SHAMAIN EDNESS, a writer, mentor, motivational speaker, and evangelist for Christ. Speaking Truth, Changing Perception, and Gaining Lives to Christ by sharing her testimonies and word of God. She is from Newark, New Jersey and partially raised in Atlanta, Georgia. She found her passion through her pain, and then her pain directed her to her God's given purpose. She is truly an inspiration to others and she gives all the recognitions to Jesus!

Shakisha Edness is the CEO/Founder of TRA-C Inc., which is named after her beloved mother Tracie. TRA-C Inc. was founded in 2006. A nonprofit organization that is designed to educate and empower men, women, and children that are affected directly and indirectly by HIV/AIDS and drug/alcohol abuse. She has mentored men in Atlanta group homes sharing her testimonies and have mentored the youth of Paulding County Public School System.

She is also the CEO/Founder of Women Overcoming Weight-loss, which has touched the lives of many women, since it was founded in 2009. She ministers to women on a daily basis through a conference call prayer line, where she has seen blessings and miracles take place in many lives.

Shakisha became an Adolescent Peer Counselor under Sandra Mc Donald, the Founder of Outreach, Inc. Working side by side with her mother at age fifteen, sharing her story of an addict's child. Shakisha since then has pursued her career in motivational speaking, evangelizing, and writing to minister to those she may never get a chance to meet.

Shakisha is an extension of God's love without limits.

AUTHOR CONTACT INFORMATION

To purchase books, for more information, or to schedule Shakisha Edness to speak, please contact:

Shakisha Edness

www.shakishaedness.com

UPCOMING BOOKS BY
SHAKISHA SHAMAIN EDNESS

Women Overcoming Weight-loss Book
Women Overcoming Weight-loss Journal
Women Overcoming Weight-loss Workbook
Break Through Volume I
Break Through I & II Workbook
Uncovering Me through Poetry
A Christmas to Remember
From the Eyes of a Child
A Man Can Only Do What a Woman Allows

NOTES

NOTES

www.ingramcontent.com/pod-product-compliance
Lightning Source LLC
LaVergne TN
LVHW051816080426
835513LV00017B/1974